FIRST
GARDEN

INTRODUCTION BY
TRUMAN
CAPOTE

DRAWINGS BY
CECIL
BEATON

DESIGNED BY
BEA FEITLER

RIZZOLI
NEW YORK

First published in 1976 by G.P. Putnam's Sons, New York

This edition published in the United States of America
in 2003 by Rizzoli International Publications, Inc.
300 Park Avenue South
New York, NY 10010

2004 2005 2006 2007 / 10 9 8 7 6 5 4 3 2 1

Printed in the United States of America

ISBN: 0-8478-2602-3

Library of Congress Control Number:

Jacket design by Sara E. Stemen

CONTENTS

I t's hard to believe that almost thirty years have passed since the original edition of *First Garden* was published. It's not surprising, however, that this simple gardening primer is still in demand today. Although I've written several books and garden planners since then, it's always *First Garden* that people want to talk to me about at my lectures.

I am extremely proud that *First Garden* has meant so much to so many people, because writing it meant so much to me—it changed my life. I had always been an athlete. I figure-skated, played tennis, fox-hunted, and competed with my horses all over the country at the highest level. One day, I was out exercising one of my horses when suddenly he jumped and whirled sideways, smashing my leg against a post. There was a nail sticking out of the post that left a four-inch gash in my leg. I had to get stitches and stay off my leg for several weeks. It was spring, and I had so much pent-up energy that I decided to write down some notes about my other passion—gardening. People always called to ask me gardening questions. When I had the idea of writing a simple garden book I wasn't sure if I could do it. But Truman Capote, my very good friend at the time, said to me, "C.Z. dear, you can do anything you set your mind to." He pushed me to have the courage to write that first book. Without his encouragement I probably would have never started my second life. The success of *First Garden* led to garden columns in the *New York Post* and *Newsday* (L.I.N.Y.), a syndicated column (for the Copley News Services in San Diego), other books, gardening planners, nationwide lectures, television appearances, presentations on QVC, and a line of candles and room sprays for Neiman-Marcus and Bergdorf Goodman. When I was too old to be a competitive athlete I was busier than ever, thanks to *First Garden*.

I have reread *First Garden* many times over the years, but when Rizzoli decided to reprint it they asked me if there were any changes that should be made. After reviewing the book in detail I realized that the only part that needed to be changed was page 41, which lists chemical pesticides. Of course we don't use chemical pesticides anymore—everything is organic. Other than that the system of gardening laid out in *First Garden* is still the same as it was then, and will be the same forever. All things that last are based on a solid foundation with rules that are tried and true, and have proven to be correct over many years of testing.

My intention in writing *First Garden* was to give people a simple system of gardening that would allow them to have fun, be successful, and gain a sense of pride and accomplishment. It's so important in today's busy world to find time to spend outdoors and enjoy nature.

And I still say, having a garden is like having a good and loyal friend. The more time and love you put into your garden, the more you will get in return. Learn to garden with this book. It's easy and fun.

Though I've wandered along many a shady lane, and down several primrose paths, I can't pretend to know much about gardening. However, I know quite a lot, more than she might prefer, about the author of the present volume, Mrs. Winston F. C. Guest. Otherwise known as C.Z. Or sometimes Cee-Zee. Actually, her name is Lucy; but the only person who occasionally calls her that is her husband.

The first time I saw Mrs. Guest was during the entr'acte on the opening night of *My Fair Lady*. Escorted by Cecil Beaton, the play's costume-designer, she was standing at a bar across from the theatre. There were fifty-odd fashionable ladies crowded there, but one could not have overlooked this one.

As Raymond Chandler remarked of his femme fatale in *The Long Goodbye:* "There are blondes, and then there are blondes." Mrs. Guest, shimmering in the blue smoky light, was one of the latter. Her hair, parted in the middle and paler than Dom Pérignon, was but a shade darker than the dress she was wearing, a Main Bocher column of white crêpe de chine. No jewelry, not much makeup; just blanc de blanc perfection.

Mr. Beaton introduced me to her, a gesture she acknowledged with ice-cream reserve. Who could have imagined that lurking inside this cool vanilla lady was a madcap, laughing tomboy? Well, I suppose anyone who knew her background: a trimly, tautly brought up Boston girl, the daughter of a Brahmin, she left Society for stage and films and, finding no satisfaction there, went adventuring in Mexico, where Diego Rivera painted her, aged twenty-two, as a honey-haired odalisque *desnuda:* a famous portrait that, according to legend, adorned a bar in Mexico City. Oh it must have been fun—but at heart she was too conservative, too *countrified,* for all that—she needed a home and a husband and dogs and horses and children (in that order) and flower gardens and vegetable gardens; and when she met the right man, the very massive but very gentle Winston F. C. Guest, she got them: houses, with gardens galore, in Old Westbury, Middleburg and Palm Beach.

Actually, when C.Z. first mentioned to me that she might be writing something, it didn't occur to me that the something would be about her horticultural concerns; I thought it would be about horses and dogs, for whom she has an animalistic affinity—indeed, I have never seen another human as at ease with dogs, as affectionate and yet in command, as Mrs. Guest. Soon, after we became friends, she invited me to visit her in Florida, and I remember watching her every morning hauling along the beach with nine and ten dogs at her heels— dogs who had nothing in common except single-hearted

devotion to their blonde friend. *Honestly,* to use C.Z.'s favorite expletive ("Honestly, now I ask you, *honestly*"), you never saw such a confoundingly assorted gang—the purest-bred English Mastiffs, mutts from the pound, an Egyptian *Saluki,* a Golden Labrador with a blind patch over one eye, a fat Peke huff-puffing to keep up, and, *everybody's* particular buddy, including his fellow dogs, a big-sized Mexican Hairless that Winston had brought home after finding him abandoned in some Godforsaken Mexican airport; what made this dog so memorable, aside from his excitable Latin wit, was that he had only three legs: a hit-and-run driver had cost him one of the frontal two. Yet it made no difference—he was right there in full-flight, retrieving the driftwood C.Z. threw into the surf, and returning with it to be hugged: "Ah, good boy. Old soldier. My old soldier."

And it is enlightening, in a quiet way, and if you are lounging in the shade with a julep in your hand, to observe C.Z. exercising one of her horses. A decade or so past, *Time* magazine published an extensive article on the upper-plateaus of American "aristocracy"—or however you choose to call it; and Mrs. Guest, as the magazine's top-selected exemplar, appeared on the cover in a very formal riding habit. Cold. Soignée. The Ice-Cream Lady. Maybe so. At horse shows. Or riding to hounds somewhere in Virginia. But usually, when observed galloping across the countryside, she is wearing cowboy chaps, and a man's shirt with rolled-up sleeves. She is certainly a finely-tuned sportswoman; and quite a sport, too.

A very *good* sport—as I have every reason to know. Once, after many years of friendship had accumulated between us, we drove together from New York to California. It was a wild ride: on the road five days and nights in a car bursting with the restless activities of two huge English Bulldogs (mine), plus a big black cat named Happy (also mine). Because of the animals, and the reluctance of restaurant proprietors to entertain them, we picnicked all the way, the dogs battling with us over such roadside delicacies as Stuckey's Chili-Dogs—chili-drowned hot dogs that we washed down with quaffs of Chateau Lafitte Rothschild quaffed straight from the bottle (Mr. Guest having provided us with a hamper of festive wines for our journey). No matter the emergency—an escaped cat, a snow-storm in Arizona, an encounter with a rude sheriff at a Georgia speed-trap, running out of gas after dark on a Texas highway—C.Z. could always cope, for she has the kind of nature that is at its most graceful under pressure.

A friend once asked me: "Do you know the difference between the rich and—well, you and me? Vegetables." "Vegetables?" "Vegetables! At Babe Paley's table, or

Bunny Mellon's or Betsy Whitney's or Ceezie's—haven't you ever noticed how extraordinary the vegetables are? The smallest, most succulent peas, lettuce, the most delicate baby corn, asparagus, limas the size of cuticles, the tiny sweet radishes, everything so fresh, almost unborn—that's what you can do when you have an acre or so of greenhouses."

My friend's observation was true—a certain kind of hostess always does serve exceptional vegetables, though owning hot-houses is apparently not the answer, for most of this elegant produce is grown in ordinary, if extensive, and extensively cared for, gardens. When I asked Mrs. Guest about this, she said: "The only thing I use hot-houses for is flowers and plants. Everything else is out of doors: raspberries, tomatoes, all that."

Templeton, the Guests' small and delightful estate in Old Westbury, has two hot-houses adjoining the rose-brick main house, and it is instructive to watch the mistress of the manor wandering around their misty, subtropical interiors adjusting a hyacinth here, straightening an orchid there: she seems so . . . exotic; and, I can't say why, a bit sinister like one of those ritzy enigmatic ladies in a stylish thriller. Perhaps the atmosphere of hot-houses, the quivering green light, the verdant haze scarcely rippled by slowly turning fans, makes everyone look like that.

But, once she has stepped across the threshold that leads from the glass houses to the walled garden that contains her row upon row of edibles and lookables, the true CeeZie emerges, like a sun sliding from behind the clouds. There, with her baskets and spades and clippers, and wearing her funny boyish shoes, and with the sun-borne sweat soaking her eyes, she is a part of the sky and the earth, possibly a not too significant part, but a part. And that is what this little testimony of Mrs. Guest's is about; well, yes, it *is* about gardening—but it's also about belonging, being a part of living things: just, you might say, life itself.

TRUMAN CAPOTE
September 15, 1975

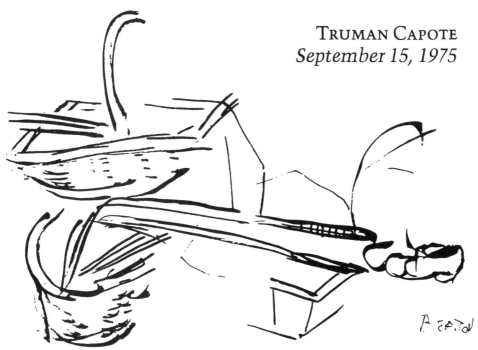

INTRODUCTION

S o many friends have been asking me questions about their gardens that I have finally decided to do something about it. I am constantly receiving phone calls from people who have seen my garden and wonder how, with my busy schedule, I am able to keep my many, many plants, flowers, and vegetables in such fine shape. I simply tell them that I have a system, and now I would like everyone to know the C.Z. system so that they may discover the beauty and pleasure of raising and tending a garden. The C.Z. system is a pattern of rules to follow which will make gardening not only easy but lots of fun. Whether you follow my rules or make your own, the important thing is that you develop a pattern. *This is the C.Z. system. This book isn't intended for any one group of people. It is for all who want to learn the ABC's of gardening and have fun doing it. The purpose of this book is to show what simple gardening has meant to me. I hope that through gardening you, too, will feel the inspiration I have felt.*

One important word that every home gardener should remember is "simplify." If your garden is overpopulated with too many kinds of flowers, it may become a huge chore instead of a delight. At my house I have two gardens, a small "formal garden" around the terrace consisting only of roses, and what is known as a "kitchen garden" of flowers and vegetables. Of course there are many plants and flowers I would like to have but don't because it would require too much maintenance. Even with help I have to oversee everything that is done since young gardeners often mistake certain flowers and vegetables for weeds. I must confess, though, when I first started gardening, I pulled up a few vegetables myself, thinking they were weeds. I chuckle at the thought now every time I show a new gardener the difference. Don't think I haven't made mistakes!

There are so many fabulous things about gardening, and the best is that absolutely anyone can do it. It's great fun, and for someone who is unhappy or lonely, having a garden is like having a good and loyal friend. Gardening can also be a tremendous relaxation for someone who is nervous. I find that being outside and using my hands to care for each flower is very soothing. In addition, once you plant your garden you'll feel such a thrill to see your things growing. Each day you'll find it's different—a new surprise! After a good rain all the young flowers and vegetables seem to sprout right out of the earth, as if to say, "Here I am!" Your garden will help you discover a whole new world. Nature can never be hurried . . . her seasons come and go—they wait for no one. There is no way you can plant a row of green beans and have them ready to eat in three weeks. You

must have a certain amount of discipline to keep your garden. If you do not take some care of it, you will find you are competing with the pests, bunnies, birds, and chipmunks. It will be a race to see who will get there first! You will also develop, as I have, a tremendous respect for nature. She can never be bullied or made to change her ways—she is truly Mother Earth. For those consumed by the pursuit and exercise of power, plant a garden—you will find one can't impress Mother Nature.

Everyone today seems to be interested in "getting back to nature." I think it's wonderful, especially for young people. We are all becoming more and more conscious of giving back to the earth what we have taken out. Gardening will make you appreciate something that many people have grown to ignore—that we are all part of the mystery of the earth's cycle of life. No scientist in the world can make winter follow spring. It's rather a relief, don't you think? Not even politicians can tamper with the seasons! Think of what a mess they would make if they could. We wouldn't know when to plant our gardens. What confusion!

A beautiful garden will give you an enormous sense of pride and accomplishment. It's great fun deciding what colors you like best and then letting your imagination run wild. I personally like orange or yellow flowers the best, and I mix all my different plants, flowers, and orchids together in my house so they never get monotonous or formal. You can get so absorbed in your gardening, and there is always something to do. You will learn from talking to other people about your garden and theirs and may also find interest in exhanging flowers and plants.

And best of all, your garden is never finished. You must keep up with it and tend to it every day. It's like watching your children grow. It will give back to you all the love and care you put into it. Your garden is a good friend—a true friend. And if you help it grow, it will never disappoint you.

FLOWERS

The other day a friend of mine called to tell me the latest news. She was in Miami Beach at a lunch party for visiting royalty, and as she strolled around the property, she thought it odd that she didn't see or hear one bird. She couldn't believe it . . . can you? It is hard to imagine a garden without birds. How sad it would be if everyone had fake lawns and flowers, don't you think? Let's start your garden now so that this doesn't happen to you.

Wherever you are, be sure that the frost is out of the ground and the soil has begun to warm up before you start. First, you must get the proper tools. I suggest a rake, hoe, shovel, garden fork, and a lightweight hose for watering. Now you must decide what size you want your garden to be. I will use the example of twelve feet by twelve feet, which I think is a good size for a beginning garden. You may go smaller, but I suggest you do not go any larger, at least for the first year, until you gain some knowledge and confidence. Decide where you want your garden and then section off that spot by taking two stakes tied together by a piece of string twelve feet long. Put the stakes in the ground , stretching the string tight. Dig a little trench under the string in a straight line. This is the first side of your bed. Make sure it is straight, or you will have a zigzag bed! Now square

DEEP PURPLE
PANSY

off your garden by doing the same thing for the remaining three sides.

You have your bed—now you can get down to business. Take your garden fork and dig. Loosen up and turn over all the dirt until it is nice and light with no grass in it. Once you've loosened the earth, get some peat moss and some dry cow or sheep manure. Mix a little of each into the soil—enough to make it porous. This fertilizer must be worked through the soil completely so that it is thoroughly mixed into the dirt. Then rake your bed to smooth it out, making sure all stones and rocks are removed. Before you plant, the soil must be thoroughly moistened a good foot down, then let dry slightly until it is workable.

Now for your first row. Take your stakes and string and make a straight line from one end of the bed to the other, a few inches from the side, and make a two-inch trench down that line. This is your first row. Take your little package of seeds and sow them along the row that you have just made. Do not bunch the seeds, so that you will have enough for two rows. Then, with your hands, lightly cover the seeds with the soil. I suggest making two rows of each flower, whichever ones you like best. You may now go onto your next row. Each row should be about twelve inches apart. Plant each row of flowers the same way. Then give your garden a watering, but very gently, so as not to wash the seeds away. Some easy-to-grow flowers that I think you'll enjoy are zinnias, marigolds, gloriosa, daisies, cosmos, sweet alyssums, sunflowers (which the birds love), and snapdragons.

To make your garden pretty, I suggest putting strawberry plants around the border. You can buy them at your local garden center, and you won't have to buy too many because strawberry plants multiply. I think eight plants will do—one in each corner and one in the middle of each row. The strawberry plants send out runners with a little plant at the end of each. In the fall you can dig up these little plants and transplant them next to their parents. In a year the perimeter of your garden will be overflowing with strawberry plants. In fact, you'll have so many you may want to give one to a friend as a present.

I would like to explain to you now the difference between annual and perennial flowers. The flowers I have suggested to you above are annuals, which means they must be replanted each year. These flowers are the most dependable because you can be sure that they'll bloom and give your garden color all summer long. When the flowers are finished, they can just be pulled out of the ground.

A thrifty trick that I use every year is this: I put yellow ribbons around the stems of the particular zinnias, marigolds, and daisies I like best. In the center of each flower there are many seeds. I let the flowers dry up on their stems, then cut off the wilted tops of the ones I have marked. I take these dried flowers, and guess where I keep them? In the attic! They stay up there laid out on cardboard until completely dried. After a month or so I put the seeds in a bag, which keeps them dry until spring planting. As a result I never buy zinnia, marigold, or daisy seeds. Try this and you will be happily surprised.

STRAWBERRY PLANT

PINK PEONY

The other flowers, called perennials, are flowers that if properly cared for can bloom for years without replanting. Some perennial flowers that I have in my garden are irises, peonies, lilies, primroses, day lilies, Oriental poppies, and sweet williams. These perennial flowers do not bloom all summer but at different times during the season. Peonies, irises, and poppies bloom in late May or early June, whereas the lilies and day lilies do not bloom until July, August, and September. Some other nice perennials that you might prefer are lupines, chrysanthemums, phlox, columbines, and delphiniums. Hollyhocks are really almost like a perennial because

SWEET
WILLIAM

AURATUM
LILY

PANSY
FORGET-ME-NOT
PRIMROSES

they reseed themselves, so I am including them in this list. Perennials can be planted in the spring, but I think that fall planting is preferable. They must be placed in a two-inch-deep hole with some peat moss or a mixed organic soil in the bottom and then covered with the dirt. The soil should be kept moist at all times.

One convenient thing about a perennial is that when the flower is finished for the season, you can just cut it down to the ground and forget about it until next year. With both annual and perennial flowers the best time to pick is in the early morning. Always pick your flowers when they are in bud (which means before they are fully opened). When picked at this time, the flowers will last longer and be more fragrant. Fresh-cut flowers absorb a lot of water, so put them in a deep vase and keep a close check on the water for the first day. Also, pull off all the lower leaves so that only the stem of the flower is immersed in the water.

I haven't mentioned roses, but I do think that everyone loves a rose. They take much more care than other flowers, so I suggest you start with just two or three bushes. Rosebushes are so easy to find nowadays. I see that they're sold in supermarkets and hardware stores, as well as in garden centers. You will find that roses are for sale continually from early spring until fall, but by far the best time to plant is in the spring. I suggest you

ROSE
(ETOILE D'HOLLANDE)

buy container-grown roses; they are slightly more expensive, but they are the easiest to plant and will bloom the soonest. Just be sure to read the directions on the package. Here is a diagram which will be very easy for you to follow.

1. Take the rose plant out of its pot, making sure the roots are undisturbed. The pot may be broken or upended. 2. The hole for your rose plant should be the same size as for a bare root plant. Make the hole at least thirteen inches across. Mix peat moss in with the soil. 3. Make a mound out of the peat-soil mixture. Place the rose plant on top of it, again making sure the roots are undisturbed. 4.

Fill up the hole carefully and water when done. Pack the soil down. 5. There is no need to mound earth around plants that have started growing in pots; this would retard their growth. Check for weak canes, removing them with a hand pruner. 6. Wait a day or two, then spray your plant with an insecticide. If not yet in bloom, it will soon start producing flowers.

Good drainage is essential in growing fine roses. Roses consume a lot of water but should not be planted where a standing pool of water can accumulate. This will kill any plant. Fertilize your roses in the spring with a little bone meal and once again in the middle of June. Then get some mulch, which can consist of many things, among which are cow manure, wood chips, leaves and pine needles, and spread it underneath the bushes at least two inches thick to keep the ground moist. When the mulch rots down, it adds to the soil an organic matter called humus, which is vital for good growth. In the spring cultivate this mulch into the soil to guarantee an increase in the humus content. Your roses must be pruned in the spring because they tend to lose their vigor after two, three, or four years and need to be replaced with young growth. Pruning concentrates growth on a select number of new shoots which are capable of producing first-rate blooms. The more severely a branch is cut back, the more vigorous will be the new growth sprouting from it. Cut the stronger shoots back eight to ten inches from the ground; all the weak and thin wood should be removed entirely.

Always begin in the spring with a clean garden. As soon as the bushes have been pruned, drench the canes, the bud unions, and the immediate soil area with a spray of fungicide-insecticide to kill overwintering, spores, and insects. Phalton, isotox, or benlate mixtures seem more effective than dormant spray and are less likely to burn. Spray immediately. Repeat in a week. After pruning them, just make sure that your roses get plenty of sun and water during the dry months, and spray once a week. Always spray in the early morning before the sun gets too hot, to avoid sunburn of wet leaves. I do it on Tuesday so that I don't forget. This is part of the C.Z. system.

Remember, it is essential that you follow some kind of pattern in tending your garden. As I said, I spray my flowers and vegetables on Tuesdays; I water them on Mondays, Wednesdays, and Fridays. Never spray your garden on the days that you water because the wet leaves will keep the spray from being effective. On the days that you water, do it in the morning so that your garden can dry off sufficiently before nighfall. If your plants are wet for a long while, they are susceptible to mildew, and roses especially are extremely prone to black spot as well as mildew. Shrub and old-fashioned roses, however, are quite hardy and resistant to diseases and bugs.

What a thrill you'll get picking your first rose. They are so beautiful.

When you cut your roses, you must do it properly to keep the plants strong and healthy. The main shoots are

MOSS ROSE

covered with thorns and small leaf-covered stems. The number of leaves on the stems varies, depending on where the stem is located on the shoot. In other words, the stems near the top of the shoot have only three leaves while stems near the middle of the shoot have five leaves and the lower stems can have seven or more. Always snip the main shoot at an angle just above the stems which have five leaves. If you pick your roses this way, you will find that new shoots will sprout from where you have cut, and your rose blooms will increase. Don't forget—you can never give your roses too much care. You will be rewarded for all your work. You will start out with a little knowledge and as you become absorbed with your garden, you will find your know-how

ROSE

GENERAL DISEASE CONTROLS

DISEASE	PLANT	TIME TO CONTROL	MATERIAL
Black spot and other fungi	Phlox, roses, perennials	As soon as detected	Phaltan or Captan
Rust	Perennials	"	Zineb or Ferbam
Blight	Peonies, fruit trees perennials	"	Botran or Benlate
Mildew	Phlox, lilacs, asters, perennials	"	Acti-dione P.M. or Benlate
Damping off	Seedlings	"	Captan, Thiram
Rot (bacteria)	Perennials	"	Agrimycin or destroy infected plants

TIGER LILY

PRIMROSES

LILY OF
THE VALLEY

increasing. And one day you'll wake up to discover you know quite a lot about gardening.

I would like to tell something interesting and useful that I found out several years ago when I imported some Duke of Windsor rosebushes from England. When brought in from other countries, flowers must go through the Agriculture Department for quarantine and inspection. There is an agricultural branch in every county. That was the first time I had ever had occasion to deal with men of the Agriculture Department, and I found them to be very nice, well educated, and helpful. These county agents came to my house three times that summer to check on the rosebushes. They told me that I was to keep any rosebushes that died so they could be burned, to ensure no spread of diseases. The men answered many questions and impressed me with their concern. I think that perhaps the Agriculture Department is the best-run branch of the government! Anyway, if you ever have any questions, I'm sure you will find the Agriculture Department to be most helpful.

One last tip. If you ever want to import various plants or orchids, you can apply to the Agriculture Department and they will issue you a number. This number is your identification and makes importing plants easier and faster for you.

ORCHID

VEGETABLES

If you want to eat well this summer, you must plant your vegetables. Again I'll use a twelve foot by twelve-foot bed as an example. You start your vegetable bed the same as you do your flower bed by sectioning it off with your stakes and string. Also use the same method to plant your vegetables as you did to plant your flowers. Again, I think it makes a vegetable garden very attractive to plant strawberries around the outside. You might also try some Bibb lettuce or parsley as a border to your garden. Some delicious vegetables for

PARSLEY

Breton

your garden are carrots, lettuce, beets, string beans, cabbage, corn, onions, and tomatoes.

There are many other vegetables which you may prefer, but the ones I have listed are the simplest ones for your first garden. Tomatoes may seem a little more difficult, but they are really quite easy to grow. There are just a few essential differences in raising tomatoes and I will explain them to you now. All of the vegetables I have mentioned can be easily started from seeds with the exception of the tomato. Tomatoes can start from seeds, but really the easiest and best way to start them

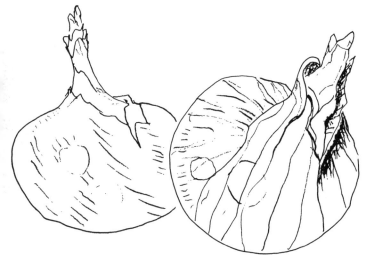

ONION

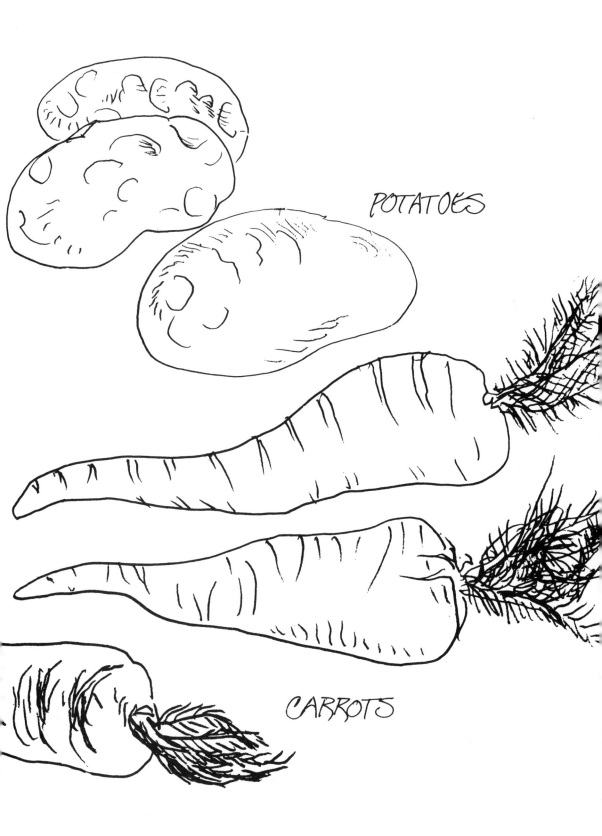

POTATOES

CARROTS

for your first garden is from small plants purchased at your garden center. Four or five plants are enough to take care of the average family for the summer. Tomatoes should be staked to grow well because if left on the ground, they will be eaten by various insects. You will need two-inch by two-inch stakes, six feet long, of

TOMATOES

cedar or redwood. Drive each stake about eighteen inches into the ground beside the plant. Plants should be twenty-four to thirty inches apart. When the plant is about fifteen inches high, tie it loosely to the stake. Each time the plant grows another fifteen inches, tie it again to the stake to keep the stem from sagging. When

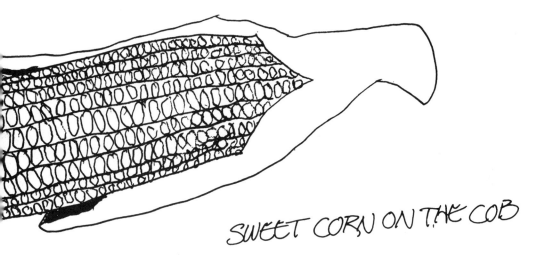

SWEET CORN ON THE COB

CUCUMBER

the plant reaches the top of the stake, you must pinch off the growing tip of the main stem for forced side branching.

Spraying of your tomatoes and all your vegetables is easy because most of the new sprays contain insecticides and fungicides which will eliminate all the garden pests and diseases. Many of the sprays come in easy sprayer-top cans. Again, it is very important to read the directions on the can, as each spray may be different. Fertilization is also easy. Your vegetable garden should be done two or three times during the summer. It is best to fertilize lightly at frequent intervals rather than one heavy dose in the spring. Commercial fertilizers contain three important chemical elements: nitrogen, phosphorus, and potash, which will enrich your soil and produce good vegetables.

A few additional vegetables to try are squash, melons, zucchini, eggplant, and lima beans. For those of you who like cucumbers, I know of the latest thing—burpless cucumbers! (I don't have to explain that one, do I?) I've been eating them all summer—it's true! You can buy them at any garden center; just ask for burpless cucumbers! Plant them, eat them, and see for yourself.

For those of you who are limited in space, such as people who live in apartments, it is very easy to grow beets, carrots, Bibb lettuce, and chard in twelve-inch redwood boxes. Just make sure the soil is moist and that there are holes in the bottom of the box for drainage. Other space savers are plants that grow vertically rather than horizontally. Use stakes and trellises for supporting vegetables such as tomatoes and cucumbers and string beans. You'll be surprised at the number of vegetables you can grow in a small space.

LETTUCE

FRUIT TREES

Fruit trees provide yet another source of pleasure—plus, they are good to eat! I think it is great fun to grow your own peaches, pears, apricots, plums, and apples. I prefer the dwarf fruit trees because they are smaller but still produce the same amount of fruit as a larger tree. You can buy these dwarf trees from a nursery and plant them in the spring. Once you have planted your trees, don't get discouraged. It is

APPLE BLOSSOM

generally advertised that fruit trees will bloom in two years, but I have found that they usually do not bloom until three to five years. The diagram below will be easy for you to follow.

1. Dig a deep, wide hole, at least six inches wider and deeper than the tree's root ball. If you are planting a large tree, make the hole even wider and deeper to ensure the new roots easy penetration. 2. Put the topsoil in the bottom when refilling (after mixing it with peat or compost), to encourage root growth. Save the subsoil for filling the upper part of the hole. 3. Put the root ball in the hole at the same depth as it was in the nursery. Measure the root ball, fill up the bottom with the topsoil-peat mixture, and place the tree. 4. Do not put fertilizer in the

bottom of the hole. Spread a ring of food around the top of the filled-in hole after planting. The plant food should be four inches from the trunk, and it should be scratched into the surface. 5. After you have filled the hole with two-thirds of the topsoil-peat mixture, water, but don't drown, your tree. 6. Build a shallow ring of soil some two inches high around the trunk about a foot out.

It is very important to spray your trees in the early spring before the buds start to come out. This kills any insect eggs which have collected on the tree during the winter. The spray is called a dormant spray, composed of lime and sulfur, and must be applied only on a mild day when the sun can dry it quickly.

You might like to have your fruit trees espaliered. I have them in my garden and find them very elegant. The prettiest gardens I have seen in Europe all have espaliered trees, and if you would like to try them, there are many nurseries that specialize in them. In case you don't know, espaliering is training a plant or small tree to grow into a definite pattern. Fruit trees are most often used because when espaliered, most of their branch surface is exposed to the sun and therefore stimulated to produce more fruit. Apples, peaches, pears, apricots, and plums are favorite espaliered trees and are a good choice to plant in your vegetable garden. Your espaliered fruit trees must be supported by a sturdy trellis because when the tree bears fruit, the branches become very heavy. Young dwarf fruit trees need very little pruning—only removal of branches that are too close together for the development of a well-balanced tree. As with all other trees, the best time to prune is in the early spring before the sap begins to run. If you happen to live in a terraced apartment in a city, why not try one or two espaliered trees in wooden tubs? They would be very impressive in a terraced garden and quite easy to care for as they are small.

There are many different ways to espalier trees; the diagram in the appendix shows you one of them.

In caring for all your your vegetables and fruit trees, remember to develop an easy-to-follow pattern. I systematically water every Monday, Wednesday, and Friday. If it is extremely hot and dry, however, and your vegetables begin to look a little "limpy," by all means water some more! Remembering: *Never, but never spray the day you water!* Mulch your vegetables as you do your flowers to keep the ground moist and also to keep the weeds down. This will save you a lot of work— weeding is such a bore. Be careful! Are you sure you are pulling up a weed?

One last point I want to make is to be sure to put a small mesh wire fence around your vegetable garden. You are not the only one who is hungry! You can imagine the disappointment you would feel after working hard to plant and care for your garden and then find that it has been eaten by someone else!

So now that everything is planted and cared for, just sit back, relax, and wait for your garden to grow!

ORANGES

PLANTS

Plants are generally kept in the house in pots. Flowering plants have become my favorites because they are so easy to care for and they are especially nice for apartment dwellers—nothing can cheer up an apartment better than a bright plant. But the *worst* and most common bad habit you can have it to overwater your plant. For some reason people think

DARK PURPLE,
RED, WHITE DAHLIA

PETUNIA

that plants have to be swimming in water. Plants are not fish! They must have a day or two to dry out or they'll drown. Do as I do—water only three times a week. Of course, in the winter they need even less watering. I mean it. *Don't overwater.* I know a really neat timesaving trick for watering. Put two or three ice cubes

ANEMONE
HYACINTH
WHITE
DAFFODIL

in the pot, depending on how big the plant is, and the water will just seep in slowly. Do this instead of dousing the plant with water. There are only a few plants that can really stand a lot of water. Two that I know of are hydrangeas and chrysanthemums.

The amaryllis is one of my favorite plants. It needs almost no care, just a little water, and no matter what you do, it seems to flower. I also think geraniums are nice. If you feed a geranium twice a month with a little plant food it can last for years. Some other nice summer plants are petunias, begonias, agapanthus, gloxinias, and impatience. There are also some nice late fall and winter plants, such as chrysanthemums. They come in many different colors, shapes, and sizes, even dwarf for those who like small flowers. Many lovely prepotted bulbs available at garden centers are especially prepared to bloom at Christmastime, such as narcissus, hyacinth, and crocus. These will last several weeks and require only a little watering. After your bulbs have finished blooming, do not cut the foliage, as it is food for the plant the following year. It is best to let them dry up completely in the pot. Do not throw them out! If you can keep them, they can be planted in the ground in the fall and will bloom the following year—or give them to a friend who lives in the country. I like doing this so that someone else can enjoy them.

PINK DAHLIA

POLYANTHUS

BrAToN.

AMARYLLIS

BEATON.

BULBS

For those of you who want to prepare your own soil and plant your bulbs from scratch in pots, I find it best to mix together equal amounts of potting soil, topsoil, peat moss, and perlite. This mixture has sufficient nutrients for plant growth and development and should be easy to work and easy for the plant roots to penetrate. All bulbs are planted in the fall and will bloom the following spring, whether they are started in pots or planted outside in the ground. Daffodils, tulips, hyacinths, crocuses, freesia, and narcissus should be potted in eight- to ten-inch pots. In the bottom of each pot put pieces of broken clay pots or stones for drainage, and then fill the pot with this mixed soil a

WHITE
HYACINTH

little above half. Put in six to eight bulbs so that they almost touch one another—be sure the pointed tips are up—then cover the bulbs with soil until the tips are just slightly under the surface. Leave an inch below the rim

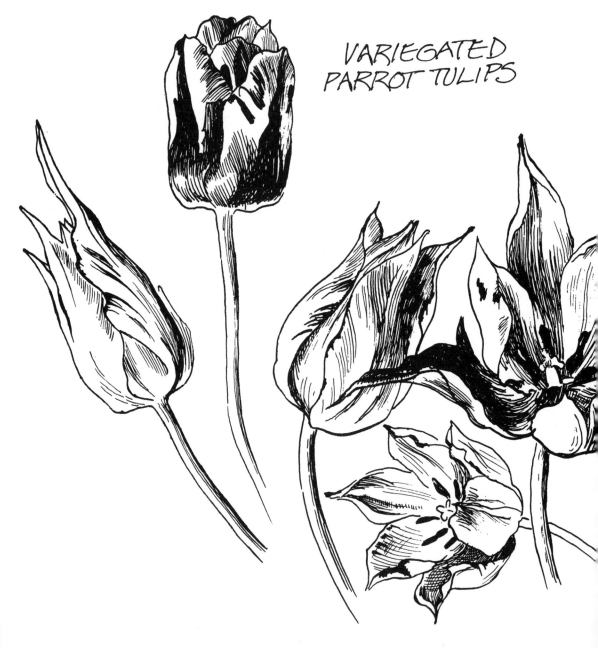

VARIEGATED PARROT TULIPS

of the pot, then water your plant thoroughly. Now that the bulbs are planted, place the pots outside and cover them with two inches of sand. Leave them outside for the winter because the cold air will stimulate the roots

RED DOUBLE
TULIP

to grow. If you have rodents around your house, you should protect the bulbs by putting a covering of mesh wire over each pot.

In the spring, when your little plants stick their heads out of the sand about two inches, it is time to bring them in. Shake or lightly brush off all the sand. The newly exposed plant is very delicate and can't stand a lot of sun right away, so it is best to put all the plants off in a corner and cover them with newspaper for about two weeks. During this time they should be watered slightly twice a week. After two weeks you can take the newspaper off and place your plants near a sunny window. Continue watering twice a week and just wait for all your beautiful flowers to bloom. If everything goes well, you'll have lovely flowers for Easter. As I mentioned earlier, when your flowers are finished, you can replant them outside in your garden. Old bulbs or any new bulbs should be planted in the ground in the fall according to the chart below.

Bulbs do not all come up at the same time. Some bloom in very early spring, while others can bloom up to three months later. I've worked out a list which will give your garden blooming bulbs from March to June.

Earliest tulips are Fosteriana, Single Early, Greigii, and Greigii Hybrids. You'll find Temple of Beauty, Red Riding Hood, and Oriental Splendor in this early

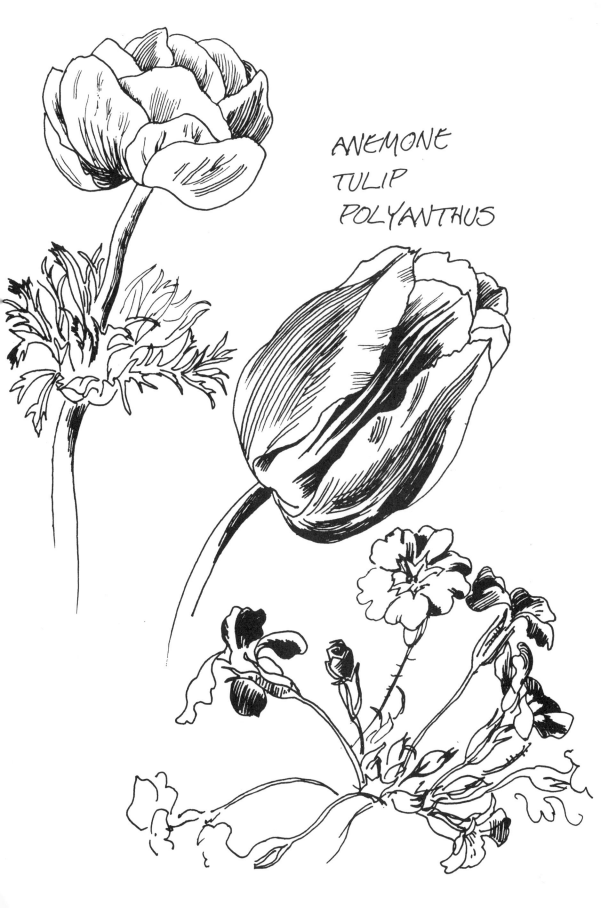

ANEMONE
TULIP
POLYANTHUS

Benton

DAFFODILS

CLEMATIS

group—they're best suited for rock gardens, early cutting beds, borders, pots, and planters. They'll bloom soon after your super-early winter buttercups, crocuses, hyacinths, and daffodils.

Next come the mid-season tulips—Darwin Hybrid, Triumph, Mendel, and some Greigii Hybrids. For splashes of bright color, plant these two inches apart. They are most effective in beds of all one variety.

The beautiful late tulips—Darwin, Cottage Parrot, Lily-Flowered, and Fringed—reach their peak in May and are especially colorful for cutting.

Double Date, or Peony-Flowered tulips, linger longest of all—these double-flowered tulips have sturdy stems and are ideal for mass plantings, borders, as well as for cutting.

I think it is fun to have a few potted herbs in the kitchen. Keep them in a sunny window and you will have herbs for cooking all year round. If you want, in the summer you can always transplant your herbs outside into your vegetable garden. I like chives, basil, rosemary, mint, oregano, savory, and sage. All of these will grow beautifully in your kitchen window as long as they have a few hours of sun each day. Again, don't overwater. Also available in pots at some garden centers are miniature lime, lemon, and orange trees, particularly nice because of their lovely fragrances.

THYME

SAGE

ROSEMARY

FLATS

There are certain advantages in starting your seeds indoors in flats. (I use discarded egg cartons.) It is the best method to use for expensive or fine seed or seeds that take a long time to germinate and grow (including most perennials). Flats can be good for some annuals and vegetables that you want to start while the ground outside is still too cold or wet. In flats you can control the soil mix and place the plants where they will get just the right amount of sunlight or shade. There is also very little danger of insects.

Flats are usually four inches high and should be filled with potting soil about halfway. Be sure there are holes in the bottom of the flat for drainage. With a pencil, mark off your rows in a straight line, pushing the pencil into the soil about one-half inch. The rows should be two inches apart. You may plant any seeds you like in any order, but I suggest planting one kind of seed per row and then using garden markers to label each row. Cover the seeds lightly and gently dampen the soil with a syringe so as not to wash them away. The soil should be kept damp. Then cover the surface of the flat with a pane of glass or a wet newspaper to keep the moisture in. Put the flats in a warm spot but not in direct sun. Try to control yourself—don't peek for four or five days! In about a week your little seeds should appear. When they've come up about one-half inch, remove the glass or newspaper and move them into an area of filtered sunlight, as they are still too tender to take full sun. In eight to ten weeks they will be ready to be transplanted wherever you want them.

In case you are not aware, there are many new, ingenious short cuts to this method. You can buy seed-starter kits that have compact nutrient-filled containers, with the seeds already planted. All you do is remove the lid of the container and water. Everything has been done for you. You can also buy what are known as Jiffy Pots. Seedlings started in them can be planted, pot and all, in the ground at the proper planting time. The roots will grow right through the soillike walls of the pot. I really think that these new methods are the best—they make starting seeds extremely easy and I suggest that everyone try them. This is what I do.

A nother fairly recent development is the method of growing plants with a fluorescent light. It is just like owning a greenhouse— you can grow anything, any time of year, by merely turning the lights on or off. Thirteen to sixteen hours of light are sufficient for most plants to bloom, but some need as much as eighteen hours. You can really grow anything you like—bulbs, seedlings, begonias, orchids, or perennials. With Gro-Lamps you have complete control of soil, moisture, and light conditions. For prime growing conditions you should have a timer switch which turns the lights on and off automatically. This will make sure the plants get the right amount of light daily, even if you are away from home. On a Gro-Lamp stand with plastic trays you can put hundreds of little plants in a small place. It is really an enchanting way of having a garden right in your living room all year round.

Of course, another great way to grow plants or nearly anything you want out of season is with your own greenhouse or lean-to. A lean-to is the most economical because it needs only three sides, the fourth side being your own house, which provides heat. Lean-tos are made of glass and are really just a small greenhouse. They should be erected on the sunniest side of your house. The best kind of lean-to is the one with aluminum frames that need no maintenance. They can easily be put up by a carpenter, or if you happen to be ambitious, you could probably do it yourself, since directions and diagrams are included with the lean-tos. They come in any size desired and can be ordered with a number of optional devices to make your indoor gardening quite easy and delightful, such as automatic ventilation systems, sprinkling systems, fans, and humidifiers. The most important thing to remember if you do have a greenhouse is *cleanliness.* Cleanliness is one of the greatest enemies to all plant diseases. Pests love rotting and decaying leaves, slime and slush, also rotting sawdust and shavings. I use fresh gravel for the greenhouse floor. If you have wooden benches, they should be made of redwood. When your plants are moved outside for the spring, nothing beats galvanized piping and galvanized steel mesh for clean, disease-free benches. Of course, you can have brick or concrete walks, but they are more expensive. That is why I suggest gravel.

A greenhouse is almost the same as a lean-to but more expensive because it is a separate building and must be heated separately. I have two greenhouses, which are heated by oil. One greenhouse is just for orchids. It is in several sections, each section housing different species of orchids; for instance, one section is just for cymbidiums and another is for cattleyas. Luckily, most orchids can be grown together in the same climatic condition, and even if they're a little different, they will usually adapt themselves. My second greenhouse is also in sections. One area is just for my acid-loving plants, such as hydrangeas, hibiscus, azaleas, and camellias with another section for growing seeds, bulbs, and plants. I get so much enjoyment from my greenhouses—in fact, I practically live in them, especially in the late fall and winter and, naturally, around Christmastime. For one who loves plants as much as I do, it is the most delightful way to pass the day or, better yet, the year.

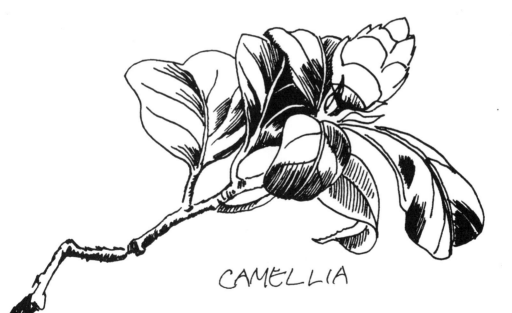

CAMELLIA

LAWNS

I swore to myself that I would not mention lawns in my book, because there is nothing more exasperating in this world than trying to grow a beautiful lawn. Several people have asked me about lawns, however, so I will just say this: It's for the birds! No matter what you do or how much you work or how much money you spend, you can never completely get rid of crabgrass—mainly because the birds carry the seeds on their wings and feet from one place to another. I've found it's an endless battle. I suggest that you just plant your lawn and do the best you can. There are so many books on lawns that I just don't want to discuss them. The more I try to kill my crabgrass, the more it grows. If you want to be happy with your lawn, do as I do. I just adore my crabgrass!

SHRUBS AND BIRDS

No house or garden is complete without shrubs. There are shrubs for every climate, so everyone should have some. They can be of many different shapes and sizes—some are green and some are flowering. I like the flowering shrubs best. Around my house I have Exbury and Knaphill azaleas in brilliant colors of yellow and orange, and I have Azalea Schlippenbachii around the stable, which have beautiful rose-pink flower clusters, because my racing colors are red and old rose. I also have some lovely lilacs in my garden. There are two new and rare varieties of lilacs from Korea, and because of their origin, they are extremely hardy and will do well in all parts of this country. They are ideal for small gardens or small properties, as they never grow more than three feet high. They are called dwarf Korean lilacs, and the two varieties with which I am familiar are Miss Kim and Palibiniana. They are very unusual because they bloom later than other varieties of lilacs. Miss Kim is an ice blue and Palibiniana is a deep red. Both have a heavenly fragrance.

My favorite hydrangea is the Paniculata Grandiflora. Its flowers start out white and gradually change to a bronzy pink as the shrub ages. It is a Japanese variety and is extremely hardy, as are the azaleas. The hydrangeas and azaleas both need an acid soil, plenty of humus, and a deep mulch all year round. They do well in full sun. One of my favorite shrubs is the Mock Orange, which has a divine fragrance—old-time gardeners sometimes call it Sweet Syringa. There are many varieties of Mock Orange, and one is as pretty as the others. Here

WHITE CAMELLIA

LILAC

are four. Enjoy a fragrant spring, summer, and fall with these varieties: Clethra Ainfolia Rosea, Enchantment (best double Mock Orange), Syringa Maude Notcutt lilac (white), and Syringa Daphne lilac (pale-pink flower). Another favorite is Hypericum Sungold, which has a lovely yellow flower but not much scent. Of course, I adore Hybrid Hibiscus with flowers of orange, red, or yellow, but unfortunately they are not hardy here on Long Island. In the summer I keep a few in pots around the terrace. Then in the fall they go back into the greenhouse. I do have some, though, at my house in Florida, planted around the tennis court. One of the first and loveliest shrubs to bloom in spring is the flowering quince. A pretty variety is called Pink Lady. It grows to only five or six feet, so it would be perfect for a small garden. Another shrub, not often seen is the hardy Daphne Somerset. It is very easy to grow and has a wondrous fragrance. This shrub is quite hardy and needs little protection from the winter, but it does like a warm location in well-drained soil. There is a lovely Daphne Genkwa which flowers in various shades of blue. This variety is ideal for flower borders, rock gardens, or in front of shrub borders, since it grows only three feet high.

There are other varieties of shrubs which produce berries. The birds simply adore them! Please don't forget the birds. Pyracanthea-Firethorn is one of my favorites because its orange-scarlet berries stay on the bush well into the winter and provide food for the birds. Viburnum Opulus Xanthocarpum produces golden-yellow berries in immense clusters and also feeds the birds well into winter.

If you have a small garden, you will naturally want to plant small shrubs. Here they are. Cydonia Knaphill, Forsythia Lynwood Gold, Spiraeas Snowbound, Hydrangea All-Summer Beauty, Hypericum Sungold, and Caryopteris Heavenly Blue will give your garden color all spring, summer, and fall, and each is only three to four feet high. All the shrubs I have named should be planted just like small trees, so consult your planting chart for directions. Shrubs are quite simple to care for, needing only to be fertilized in the spring and fall and kept well mulched.

There are several shrubs that flower in the fall but are not often seen. One is Stewartia Pseudo-camellia, which has beautiful white fragrant flowers; because of the form of its blossoms, it is often referred to as imitation camellia. In the late fall the foliage turns to a red and golden yellow. Cornus Kousa Chinensis (Milky Way) is another fall bloomer and has large strawberrylike fruit and scarlet foliage.

I do not want to forget to mention vines and vinelike

FORSYTHIA

climbing shrubs. They provide beauty where no other plant can. They are especially useful in camouflaging unsightly fences and buildings, and they require almost no ground, space, or care. You really do not see vines too much in America, but in England even the smallest cottage gardens have them winding up a wall or fence. I have two vines in my garden which bloom throughout the summer. Each is a different variety of Bignonia—(Campsis) Trumpet Vine. One is Madame Gallon—the flowers are a rich apricot tinted orange with a fine dark-green foliage. The other is Yellow Trumpet with flowers of apricot yellow. They are both perfectly hardy and immune to all insects. They grow fast and need no support, as they fasten themselves easily to any fence or wall. Another beautiful vine which does especially well on walls is the clematis, of which there are many different varieties. Mountain Rube is an early-blooming pink vine, whereas Clematis Paniculata is a late bloomer, flowering in August and September. My favorite is the Clematis Tangutica, which comes from China. It has masses of yellow flowers and it blooms all summer through fall. There are also some lovely hybrids available which are very different and fun to have. When planting your vines, the most important thing to remember is that the hole should be dug one foot away from the wall or fence—never any closer. The hole for

CRIMSON
ROSE

ROSES

the clematis should be several inches larger and deeper than the size of the roots. This extra room provides a good root run for our vine, enabling it to grow well and produce many more flowers. Once the vine is planted, three-quarters of the top growth should be cut back and the remaining crown covered with two or three inches of earth. Then just add a light mulch to keep your vine moist. It will be the envy of all your neighbors!

One final thought . . . for those of you who go to the country during the summer, take your plants with you so that they can have a vacation, too. If you live in the country, put your plants outside for the summer. They love the fresh air and sunshine just as you do. An important thing to know is that the morning sun is the very best sun for your plants. The afternoon sun can burn the leaves, so if possible, shade your plants in the afternoon, especially during the hot, dry months of July and August. Then, in the fall when the nights get below sixty degrees, take your plants inside. Spray them first to get the bugs off. You will be amazed how much they have grown.

Since I've mentioned birds several times in this chapter, I feel that this is a good place to tell you how to make more little friends. Many people think that they need to put out bird feed only in the winter. This is not true. In the spring and summer there is very little natural food available to the birds. It is not until fall that the birds find the necessary wild seed in nature. If you want a wide range of birds in your garden, put out bird feed all year round. There are a variety of feeds available to attract a variety of birds. In addition to food, birds also appreciate water and birdbaths. After all, we all love to bathe! In the winter especially, birds suffer from a lack of water because everything is frozen. You can easily buy a little birdbath heater which will keep your birds happy and healthy, and the feed you put out will keep them warm in the frozen months of the year. (The feed keeps the birds fat, which insulates their bodies in the winter.) In my garden I have several different feed stations. I also have a wonderful window feeder, attached directly to the window, which enables me to see my little birds even when I am inside. As well as feed stations, I have several bird houses around my garden. You know, birds have housing problems just as we do! To solve my birds' problems I rely on the Audubon Society. They have many attractive bird houses for various kinds of birds. There are big houses and small houses, because all birds *can't* live together. Most birds have their own territories, but there are always a few big bullies lurking around. Little birds need their little houses to escape such a menace. The Audubon Society has just the right housing for everyone.

THE WAY I USE FLOWERS

I really have no set plan on how to arrange flowers. I love all different flowers together, and I find that almost all flowers and plants compliment one another. As I said before, I prefer orange and yellow flowers, but at Christmastime I love festive red and white ones. I also do something that very few people would ever dream of doing. I mix orchids with other flowers. They are really the most beautiful of all—each is unique and individual and they come in different shapes, colors, and forms. And some are almost too beautiful for words. I never tire of looking at one. They are usually quite easy to grow, but orchids can sometimes be like people—some need to be pampered more than others. You probably have the idea that orchids are quite expensive; it's not true! I know a commercial-orchid grower in Florida who has a fantastic idea. His greenhouse is like a supermarket. Inside the door are three large tables just packed with multicolored, multishaped orchids, each table having a different price range. You can study and compare all of these beautiful orchids and then choose the one or ones you like best, ranging in price from only $5 up to almost $25. Fortunately, or unfortunately for me, I pass by this marvelous place each day on my way back from riding my horses. I almost always have an irresistible urge to stop in . . . just to look around, of course. I really cannot help myself—I buy one or two. So you see, by the end of the season I have quite a collection. Once you get interested, you will find that the hobby of collecting orchids is a never-ending quest. A few of the species I like are paphiopedilums, cymbidiums (also miniature), epidendrums, dendrobiums, calanthes, miltonias, oncidiums, renantheras, zygopealtum, vandas, and cattleyas.

Everyone can afford to buy an orchid plant, and I think that everyone should. Just for fun, go out and buy one and see what happens. It can be quite a challenge to get your orchids to bloom every year, and when you become a really good gardener, you may even be surprised and get them to bloom twice a year. In every big city there is an orchid society, and if you call, I'm sure they will be only too happy to give you advice on caring for your orchid. You may make some new acquaintances. I have. Who knows, you could become a hobbyist just like me!

Getting back to arrangements, I love and use lilies quite a bit. The colors and varieties are incredibly beautiful, especially the Oriental lilies from Korea and Japan. I often arrange them in tall bottles of different sizes, shapes, and colors that I collect on my travels to Europe. I also collect various baskets as containers for my plants. I think that a plant looks more dressed up when it's set inside a basket. I often put a vase of roses on a ta-

ble with lilies or with an orchid plant. An amaryllis next to a hydrangea is quite pretty, as well as an amaryllis with a geranium. The height of the amaryllis makes it a choice companion in an arrangement, especially with rather short, bushy plants. Or try an amaryllis in a basket with lilies of the valley around it. They come in lovely shades of red, white, pink, and even orange. In your arrangements, as well as contrasting and matching colors, you can contrast and match sizes and shapes. That is what I do, and the combinations are dazzling. Clivia plants, which are bulbs, are another favorite of mine. They are a spectacular orange color and make a very impressive showing on any table. Clivia plants come from Borneo, so they are fairly difficult to find, but if you ever have the chance to buy one, do, and you'll never be sorry. For your lunches or dinner parties I suggest a low cut flower or plant—maybe even an orchid—so that you can see across the table. As I have said, you can let your imagination run wild. Last week I discovered a fabulous new arrangement for one room in my house by placing some of the new Envy zinnias in two K'ang Hsi frogs (Chinese porcelain) at each end of a coffee table. In the center I put a tall cattleya orchid. The Envy zinnias are a lovely light green and the cattleya is pale lavender with a yellow throat—together they are exquisite! I then put several more orchids of the same color on the other tables in the room and then added yellow zinnias in vases. To my surprise, the effect was spectacular! And I had great fun creating it. If you have an outdoor patio, potted geraniums, hydrangeas, daisies, or jasmine can be a gay addition. Some people like roses in pots. Even miniatures are pretty. I suggest dwarf fruit trees, which I think look prettiest in wooden tubs. For the bedroom I prefer roses in a vase or a few small orchid plants, but a bouquet of violets is the best. For my front hall I like big plants in baskets, such as tall lilies. Some species of orchids, such as cymbidiums, grow quite tall, and I use them as I do the lilies, lemon trees, and camellia bushes. Also standard geraniums and standard white or pink azaleas. All of these, naturally, must be in season. Maybe you could use one or all of them to make your entrance hall pretty. When I walk into someone's house and see beautiful flowers, it automatically puts me in a good mood. I think it really tells something about the people. After all, it does take some care and trouble to put them there. Why don't you try bringing plants and flowers into your Life? You will be surprised at the difference they make.

The thrill of springtime exists for everyone. I always feel sorry for those who are forced to miss it. I am so excited to see the bulbs I planted last fall pushing their noses out of the ground. Every day is a new surprise—

different species of birds arriving, fighting for their territories. Even pheasants appear on my place, crowing for their mates. And those darling little chipmunks coming out of their burrows, awakening at the call of spring. Most of us have no idea how busy Mother Earth is at this time, releasing all her family. It's almost like magic! Think how exciting the first warm day is—to hear one bird—the smell in the air—to run outside barefoot—to lie in the grass—there is electricity in the air and it is transferred to us! The renewal of life.

Everything we have the earth gives us—we take it so for granted. *Don't* let yourself miss this. Gardening is the best therapy in the world. You can put so much into it and get so much back. Love is everything. . . . How lucky we are to live on this beautiful earth—you can bring the beauty to yourselves through gardening. Your garden will help you realize and appreciate how truly exquisite nature is!

C. Z. GUEST

"Templeton," Old Westbury, Long Island, N.Y.
August 15, 1974

ESPALIERING

Training plants to grow into specific shapes and patterns is a gratifying but rigorous art, which can be applied to many kinds of plants. The illustrations below demonstrate how to espalier a fruit tree. Fruit trees are ideal for espaliering, since the process turns more of the branch surface toward the sun, thus bringing on more flower and fruit production. Pears, cherries, apricots, plums, and apples all lend themselves readily to espaliering, and dwarf versions are available for those with smaller gardens.

If your garden is in a warmer climate, give an eastern exposure to your trees so the fruit won't be burned by reflected heat. On the other hand, colder regions dictate choosing a southern site.

Make sure your supports are sturdy; when full of fruit, branches are heavy. Use posts of galvanized wood or pipe (four by four inches), and stretch fourteen-gauge galvanized wire tightly on turnbuckles. Remember to leave four to twelve inches between wall and trellis so air can circulate.

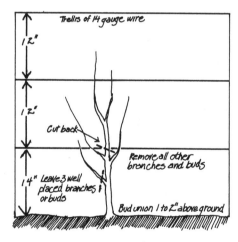

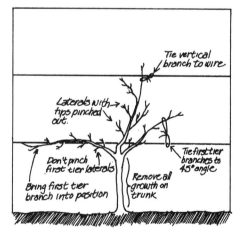

1. Planting time. Your newly planted tree is supported by a wire, strung north to south, with turnbuckles that can be tightened. Tie first-tier branches to wire; remove all others.

2. Growing season #1. Slowly train first-tier branches to grow horizontally. Tie the growing vertical branches to the next wire. Pick two young branches for next tier and pinch tips of any others.

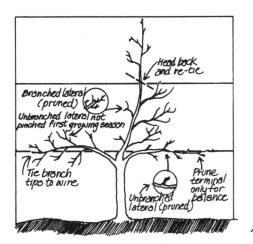

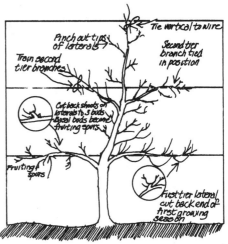

3. Dormant Season #1. Head the vertical branch back below the second wire as soon as the tree loses its leaves. Two branches should be left for the second tier, any others cut back to stubs with two or three spurs.

4. Growing season #2. The second-tier branches should be trained in the same manner as the first tier. All laterals below the second tier will produce fruiting spurs at their base, and fruit will appear in a year.

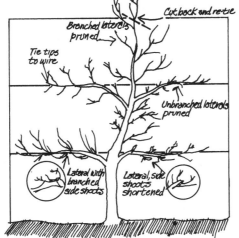

5. Dormant season #2. Head the vertical branch back below the third wire. Second-tier laterals should be pruned as were the first tier. Continue to train, keeping tree to designated shape.

PRUNING FRUIT TREES AND ROSES

The drawings below show you the correct way to prune three different kinds of roses. There are many different approaches to correct pruning, but one thing to keep in mind is this: Besides the major pruning, which happens only once a year, prune a little bit all year round. Spent flowers need to be removed, and branches that tangle and cross should be trimmed back.

As for fruit trees, cherry, apple, and pear trees need only light pruning of damaged or inferior twigs and branches. But nectarines and peaches are just the opposite. If not pruned regularly, they can easily get out of hand. Remember that last summer's new growth will produce this year's fruit and flowers. So always leave some of the previous year's new growth, else your tree will not produce fruit.

Like peaches, apricots and plums grow quickly. But like apples, their fruit is produced on slow-growing short spurs. New branches that are too straggly or long can be removed completely without the loss of the entire fruit crop. Try, though, to leave at least a piece of each new branch.

Cut spurs along canes of climbers so two or three good buds remain.
Prune standard rose to keep top open and symmetrical and to remove twigs..

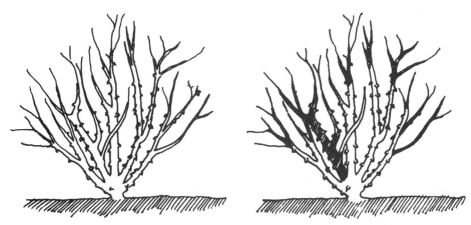

From January (in mild climates) to early spring (in cold climates) you can prune dormant rosebushes. Remove weak stems, branches that cross, and the oldest canes.

Where the winter climates are mild, cut the canes back, leaving two-thirds of the plant. Harsher climates call for a half to two-thirds to be removed.

RIGHT WRONG

Old canes should be cut flush with the bud union. Stubs will rot and can damage the entire plant.

PROFIT FROM SEASONAL CHANGE

This chart was prepared for Long Island growing seasons, but it can be made to apply to any area where first frost occurs in October and last frost in April. The harvest is extended by planting for fall and winter crops.

EARLY SPRING—Plant as soon as the ground can be worked in spring. Broccoli plants • Cabbage plants • Endive • Kohlrabi • Lettuce • Onion sets • Parsley • Peas • Radishes • Spinach • Turnips

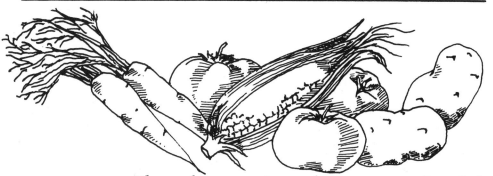

MID-SPRING—Plant these at time of the average last killing frost. Carrots • Cauliflower plants • Beets • Onion seeds • Parsnips • Swiss Chard. Plant two weeks later: Beans • Corn • Early potatoes • Tomato seeds

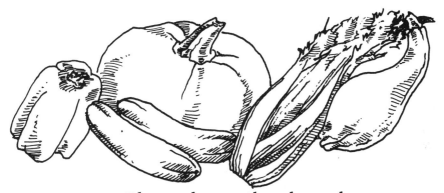

EARLY SUMMER—Plant when soil and weather are warm. Lima Beans • Cantaloupe • Celery plants • Crenshaw melons • Cucumbers • Eggplant plants • Pumpkins • Pepper plants • Potatoes for winter • Squash • Tomato plants • Watermelons

MID-SUMMER—FALL—Plant in late June or early July. Beets • Broccoli • Cabbage • Cauliflower • Kohlrabi • Lettuce • Radishes • Spinach • Turnips

WINTER PROTECTION METHODS

Make a mound of soil twelve or more inches high over the bud union of each bush (the soil should come from another part of the garden). After the mounds freeze, cover them with straw to keep them frozen.

Soil is held in place around canes by a cylinder of wire mesh, which easily lets water drain away.

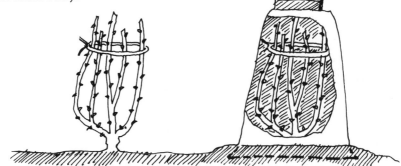

To use Styrofoam rose cones, canes must be tied together and cut down to fit the cones. A brick placed on top and soil over the flanges will hold the cone in place.

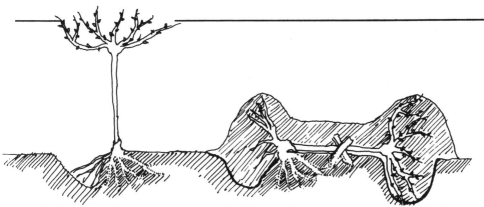

For bush roses, the "Minnesota tip": Dig up the roots on one side of the bush, bend the bush over into a trench, and cover it with soil.

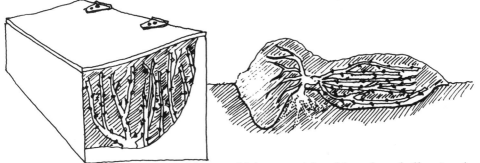

Large bushes can be protected by a cold frame with a hinged roof allowing for ventilation on warm days. Bend plant over bud union of trunk and roots, pin the trunk to soil, and cover for "tipping" standards.

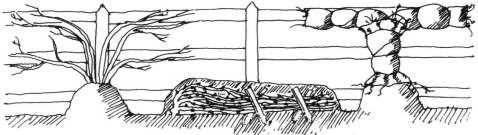

Climbers should be protected with a soil mound in areas where winter temperatures range from 5 to 15 degrees. Canes should be covered with soil if temperature drops below −10. For −10 to +5 degree weather, blanket plant with straw wrapped in burlap.

BULBS

BULBS, CORMS, AND TUBERS

These charts show the proper planting seasons for each of eighteen bulbs, corms, and tubers, as well as the depths at which each should be planted. Note also that there is a correct and an incorrect way of placing the bulbs in the ground.

SPRING FLOWERING

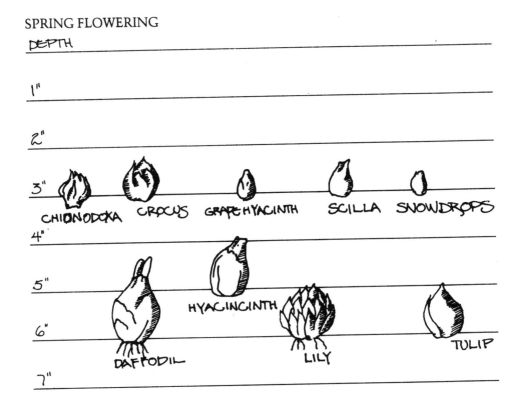

SUMMER FLOWERING

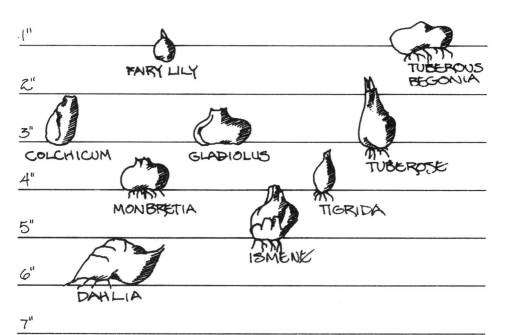

DEPTH

.1" FAIRY LILY · TUBEROUS BEGONIA

2"

3" COLCHICUM · GLADIOLUS · TUBEROSE

4" MONBRETIA · TIGRIDA

5" ISMENE

6" DAHLIA

7"

PLANTING HOLES

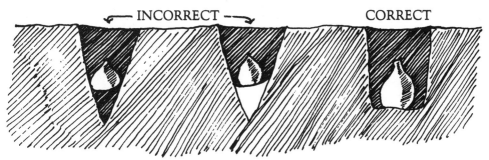

← INCORRECT → CORRECT

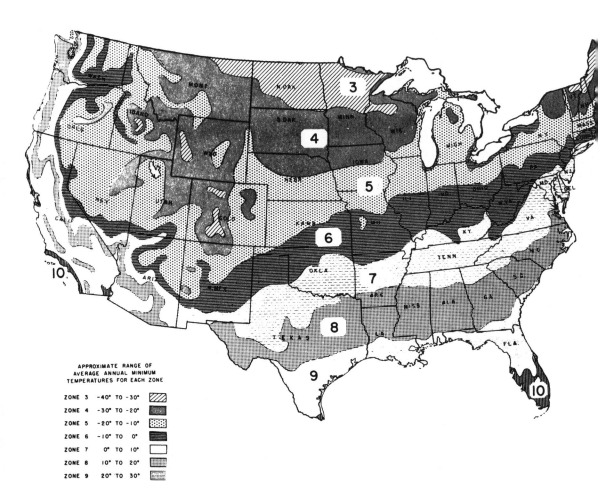

APPROXIMATE RANGE OF
AVERAGE ANNUAL MINIMUM
TEMPERATURES FOR EACH ZONE

ZONE 3	-40° TO -30°
ZONE 4	-30° TO -20°
ZONE 5	-20° TO -10°
ZONE 6	-10° TO 0°
ZONE 7	0° TO 10°
ZONE 8	10° TO 20°
ZONE 9	20° TO 30°
ZONE 10	30° TO 40°

PLANT HARDINESS ZONE MAP

The plant hardiness zone map—devised by the United States Department of Agriculture—is used in countless nursery catalogs and garden books to indicate where plants can be grown. In the map's original concept, the reader was to locate on the map the climate zone in which he lived; then, if the zone number given for a particular plant was the same as, or smaller than, his climate zone number, the plant was judged to be hardy in his locale. In our listings, we have followed the standard method of hardiness rating; but in addition to indicating the coldest zone the plant will grow in, we consider its adaptability and usefulness in the warmer zones, and indicate all zones in which the plant is generally grown.

The limitations of the map are obvious. It is impossible to accurately map local variations in climate. Furthermore, a map based on temperatures only is misleading when considering plants which have special soil requirements; for example, plants such as rhododendrons, azaleas, and pieris require acid soil, but this soil will not necessarily be found throughout their range of favorable growing climates.

INDEX